Oh No!

words by Michael Steer
illustrated by Mark Wilson

"Oh, no!" said Jo.
"There's a frog on my plate.
What am I going to do?"

"I'll feed him," said Jo.
"I'll feed him peas.
That's what I will do."

"Oh, no!" said Jo.

"There's a fish in my bath.
What am I going to do?"

"I'll wash her," said Jo.

"I'll wash her with soap.
That's what I will do."

"Oh, no!" said Jo.

"There's a bear on my bed.
What am I going to do?"

"I'll read to him," said Jo.

"I'll read him a story. That's what I will do."

The bear went to sleep.

"Oh, no!" said Jo.
"What am I going to do?"

"I'll go to sleep too.
That's what I will ... zzzzz!"